# THE NATIONAL SHRINE OF THE DIVINE MERCY

## A PILGRIMAGE IN PHOTOS

# The National Shrine of The Divine Mercy

## A Pilgrimage in Photos

*Theresa Peloquin*

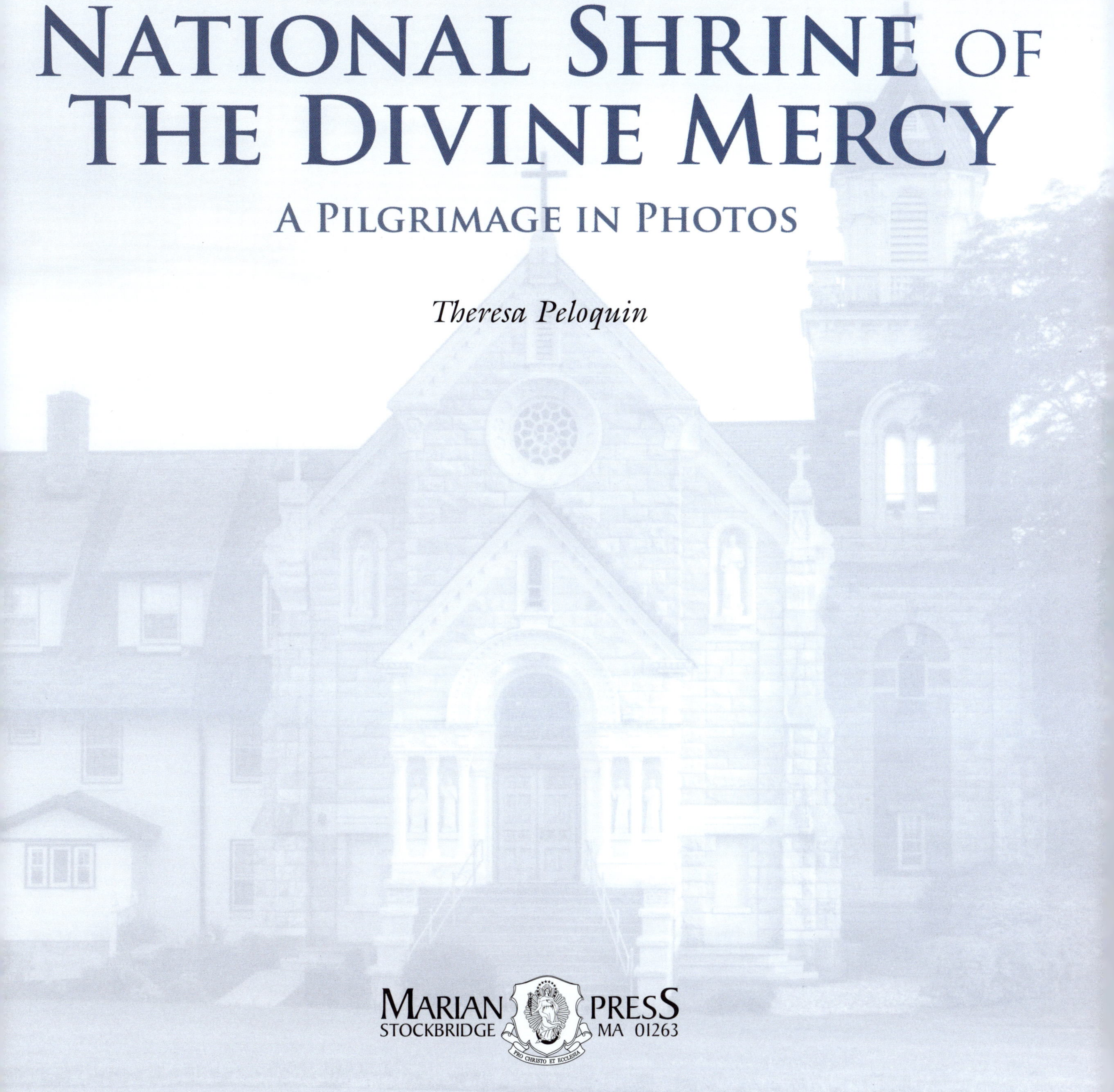

MARIAN PRESS
STOCKBRIDGE MA 01263

2020

Available from:
Marian Helpers Center
Stockbridge, MA 01263

Orderline: 1-800-462-7426
marian.org
ShopMercy.org

Publication Date:
August 3, 2020

*Nihil Obstat:*
Dr. Robert A. Stackpole, STD
Censor Deputatus
The Blessed Virgin Mary, Mother of Mercy Province
May 20, 2020

ISBN: 978-1-59614-528-3

Design by Curtis Bohner

Photographs by Felix Carroll, Br. Mark Fanders, and from the Marian Archives



Printed in the United States of America

# Contents

# Dedication

In loving memory of my godmother, Elaine DePonte,
who encouraged me to apply for a job as a writer with the Marian Fathers.

# Acknowledgements

Thanks to Mary Clark for her guidance and patience.
Thanks to Mitchell Kruszyna for his help in locating Marian Archive photos.
Thanks to Mary Kay Volpone for help in developing content.
Thanks to Felix Carroll and Br. Mark Fanders, MIC, for their outstanding photography.
Thanks to Robert Stackpole, STD, for proofing for theological accuracy.
And thanks to Curtis Bohner for the huge undertaking of designing this book.

# NATIONAL SHRINE TIMELINE

### 1739
Reverend John Sergeant, the first missionary to the Native Americans, builds a wooden frame home on the hill called "The Mission House" for his wife Abigail.

### 1855
David Dudley Field, Jr., a lawyer, law reformer, and politician purchases the property known as Eden Park and builds a summer home.

### 1906
Samuel Woodward, of Washington, D.C., builds a new English Tudor-styled home (in place of the summer home) as his family's summer cottage. He renames the plot Eden Hill and the home Eden Hall.

### 1938
The Episcopalian diocese of Albany, New York, operates St. Edmund's School for Boys at Eden Hall until 1941. The school shut down when World War II broke out and young men were being drafted.

### 1943
The Marians purchase the Eden Hill property. Bishop Thomas M. O'Leary of the Diocese of Springfield, Massachusetts, blesses the building.

### 1950
Skilled carpenter and resident of Stockbridge, Antonio Guerrieri begins to build the annex and chapel.

### 1960
The Divine Mercy Chapel is completed. The Bishop of the Diocese of Springfield, Massachusetts, officiates the blessing.

### 1985
Pope John Paul II offers a special blessing for every pilgrim who visits the Shrine of The Divine Mercy in commemoration of its 25th anniversary.

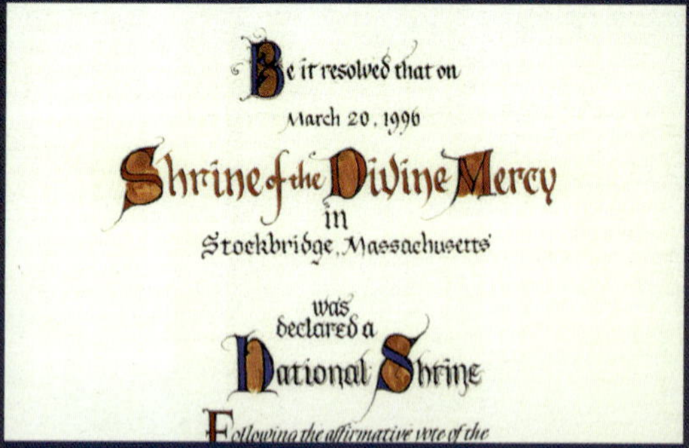
Be it resolved that on
March 20, 1996
Shrine of the Divine Mercy
in
Stockbridge, Massachusetts
was
declared a
National Shrine
Following the affirmative vote of the

### 1996
The bishops of the United States designate the Shrine as the National Shrine of The Divine Mercy.

## 2000
At St. Peter's in Rome, Pope John Paul II canonizes St. Maria Faustina Kowalska, referring to her as "the great Apostle of Divine Mercy," and declares the Feast of Divine Mercy.

## 2007
Construction begins on the Mother of Mercy Outdoor Shrine to provide a sheltered, respectful setting to accommodate pilgrims when their number exceeds available seating in the National Shrine.

## 2010
Thousands of pilgrims participate in the year-long Golden Jubilee celebration of the National Shrine of The Divine Mercy. The celebration was marked by a plenary indulgence granted by the Holy Father.

## 2012
The life-size outdoor Stations of the Cross are dedicated by Bishop Timothy A. McDonnell of the Diocese of Springfield, Massachusetts. A first-class relic of Blessed John Paul II is enshrined in a marble kneeler in the Shrine. And a new pilgrim entranceway, then called the "Blessed John Paul II Plaza" is dedicated.

## 2014
After the canonization of Pope John Paul II in 2014, the plaza is renamed "the St. John Paul II Plaza."

## 2015
A small statue of St. John Paul II is installed near his first-class relic.

## 2016
On June 5, the Marian Fathers' founder, St. Stanislaus Papczynski, is canonized. A first-class relic is enshrined in a marble kneeler opposite his fellow Polish countryman, St. John Paul II, inside the Shrine.

## 2018
The Shrine of the Holy Innocents is officially completed and rededicated. It memorializes children lost through miscarriage, abortion, stillbirth, or other cause.

# Origins

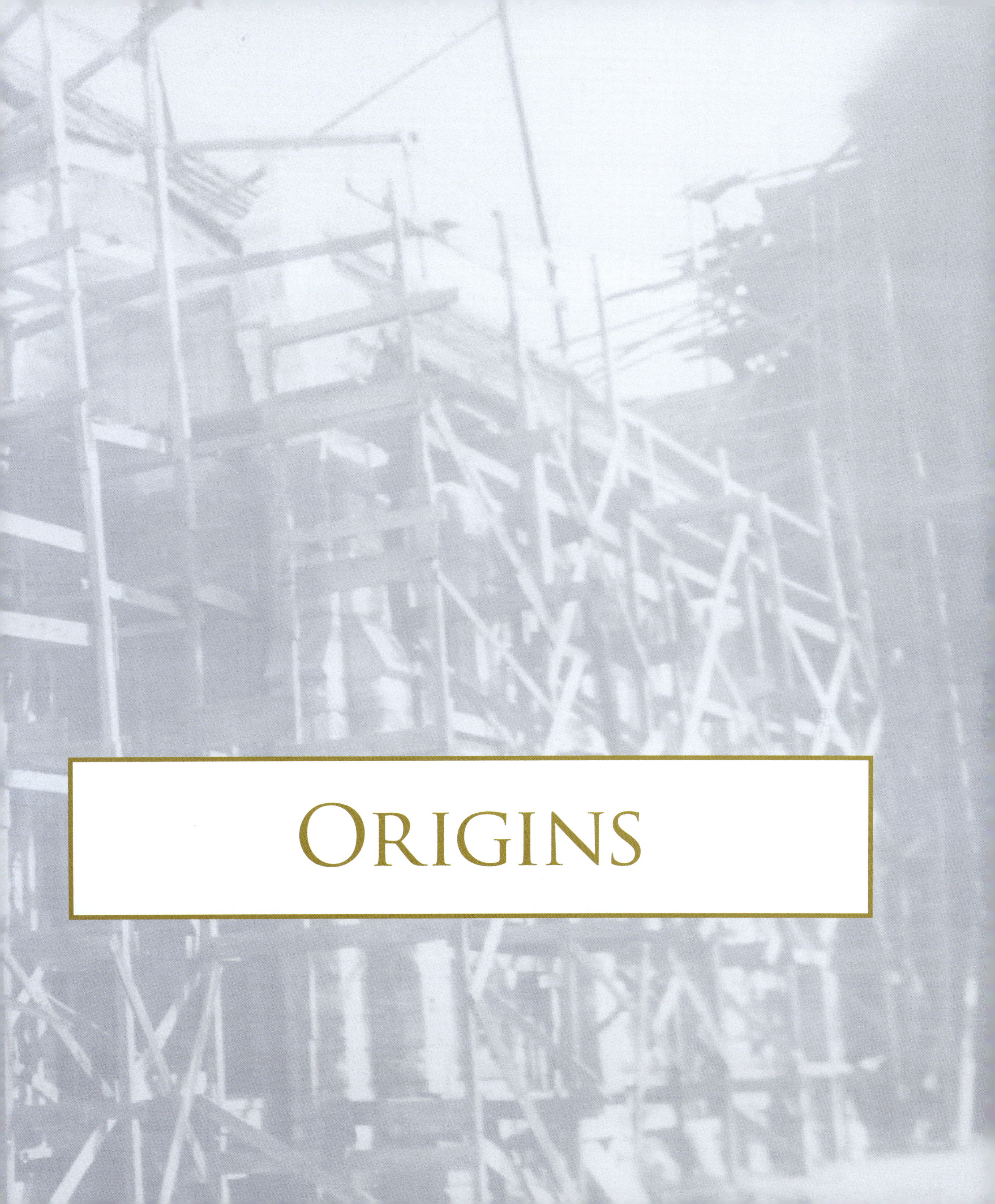

2019 Encuentro Latino

**Why Stockbridge, Massachusetts?**

Every year, an estimated 20,000 pilgrims come to the National Shrine of The Divine Mercy to celebrate Divine Mercy Sunday — the Second Sunday of Easter. Thousands more arrive throughout the year. They come to experience the peace of Eden Hill and to receive God's mercy. Many have reported miracles and healings at the site. Others come here to give thanks for graces received.

So why in the world is the National Shrine of The Divine Mercy *here* in the Berkshires, a cultural hub in the hills of western Massachusetts?

After all, it was in Poland where the spark was lit for the modern Divine Mercy movement. It was in Poland in the 1930s where the Lord revealed Himself to a humble nun now known to the world as St. Faustina, whose *Diary* has become a modern spiritual classic.

Why Stockbridge — famous as the home of artist Norman Rockwell and the musical venue Tanglewood?

The story contains heroic twists, dramatic escapes, and divine grace that resulted in the Divine Mercy message and devotion finding a beachhead here in Stockbridge. It was here, on Eden Hill, where the Marian Fathers of the Immaculate Conception undertook the task of becoming official promoters of Divine Mercy, which has since become the greatest grassroots movement in the history of the Roman Catholic Church.

It was here — home of the Association of Marian Helpers — where the message was passed from Poland.

How? Read on …

† 1931 rok 22 lutego

## The Marian Connection

Since 1941, the Marians have been official promoters of the authentic Divine Mercy message — a message that has emanated from Poland through Eden Hill into the lives of hundreds of thousands of people and thousands of parishes throughout North America and beyond. How did they receive this role?

The Polish nun, Sr. Maria Faustina Kowalska, who was chosen by our Lord to receive His revelations of Divine Mercy, died in 1938. That's when her spiritual director and confessor, Blessed Michael Sopocko (above, left) became the *de facto* bearer of her revelations.

At the time, the Nazi occupation of Poland made it difficult to speak publicly about anything — let alone God — and getting something published was out of the question.

In response, Fr. Sopocko prayed. God answered by sending him a Marian priest: Fr. Joseph Jarzebowski, MIC (above, right). This Marian told Fr. Sopocko that he was going to attempt to escape to America. Recognizing an opportunity to get the message of Divine Mercy out of Poland and to the rest of the world, Fr. Sopocko "passed the torch" of the message of Divine Mercy to Fr. Joseph.

So, with a deep trust in the Merciful Jesus, and with a document called "Memorandum on the Institution of the Feast of Divine Mercy" from Fr. Sopocko tucked into his small bag, Fr. Joseph braved the long, hard journey to America. He had to pass through border patrols, answer to KGB (Soviet secret police), cross 6,000 miles of frozen Russian land, sail from Siberia to Japan, and from there to America.

When Joseph's ship docked in Seattle, his travels hadn't ended. He had to get to Washington, D.C., where a Marian community had been established. Once he arrived, Fr. Joseph told the story of his amazing adventure, and how it happened thanks to Divine Mercy. Father Joseph firmly believed it was a miracle. He felt that Jesus wanted to grant even greater miracles to those who also would trust in Jesus' mercy.

*Many people never would have heard of Divine Mercy if it weren't for Fr. Walter (Ladislaus) Pelczynski, MIC, who arranged for the Marian expansion to Eden Hill in Stockbridge, Massachusetts.*

### The Message Spreads

From 1942, the Marians in Washington, D.C., with the help of the Felician Sisters, began to publish Divine Mercy materials, including prayers from the *Diary of Saint Maria Faustina Kowalska*, and distribute them across the country. Soon, the little Marian community in D.C. was overwhelmed by wave after wave of letters filled with testimonies to the power of God's mercy working in people's lives, and thanksgiving for the graces received through the devotion to Divine Mercy.

Enter Fr. Walter (Ladislaus) Pelczynski, MIC. He was a man known for the personal touch. His letter writing became legendary. He'd knock on doors and sit with strangers who quickly became lifelong friends and supporters of the Marians.

It was Fr. Walter Pelczynski, MIC, who would put Eden Hill on the map.

Before his ordination on May 28, 1942, he and other seminarians began corresponding with family members and others who supported their efforts. The men also formed friendships with people who had given their names at different parishes where Divine Mercy brochures had been distributed.

Still in his first year of priesthood, Fr. Walter went home for a visit in 1943. He was asked by his superiors to look for a place in the country for a novitiate (a training headquarters for the religious life). The hope was that such a place would also serve as headquarters for his Congregation's apostolic activities.

He made his way up a hillside in Stockbridge to find Eden Hill. There was a beautiful summerhouse on an old farmstead. The views were stunning.

*The Berkshire Hills of western Massachusetts.*

"This place is indeed a bit of Heaven," Fr. Walter said. "This property must be ours."

With "trembling hopes," as Fr. Walter described in his memoirs, he sought to raise funds to purchase the property. The sale price was a bargain at $22,500. He succeeded, mainly through the support of Polish-Americans from the region, all hoping to see the Marians prosper beyond the Congregation's native Polish homeland. He credited Divine Providence, but he and the Marians did the legwork.

"Within two months we had acquired the extensive property in Stockbridge that was to become our center of activities in the United States as well as missions abroad," he recorded in his memoirs. A few years later, the Marians annexed the former Turner farm, whose outbuildings and main house were readapted.

On Eden Hill, the Marians dedicated themselves to their evangelization work, including a publishing apostolate that continues to this day. They continued their correspondence with people who had shown an interest in learning more about the message of Divine Mercy as it was proclaimed by Sr. Maria Faustina Kowalska. With spiritual zeal, the Marians on Eden Hill established relationships with more and more people who were searching for spiritual nourishment. These efforts grew to become the Association of Marian Helpers in 1944. This spiritual benefit society, now some 1.5 million members strong, continues to prayerfully and financially support the Marians and their work throughout the world.

*The Marians saw God's providence in sending them Antonio Guerrieri to build the shrine. In July 1950, the Marians'* Bulletin *noted that Guerrieri "has come to aid us, despite the fact that our material means are wanting."*

*CHAPEL WORK BEGUN . . . .*

*Starting the foundation of our new Chapel*

On a calm day, in the first part of May, the tranquility of Eden Hill was disturbed by a great rumble of a steam-shovel, three trucks, and a bull-dozer. The long-awaited event of digging the foundation for our new Chapel had finally come.

In the course of five toilsome days, a great, gaping hole remained in the place which formerly was part of a beautiful lawn dotted with some very old trees.

Tons upon tons of earth were removed from the site of the Chapel which will be dedicated to the Merciful Saviour, and before long, the foundation will be laid, with the walls, roof, etc., following.

The limited means which we had in order to begin the work on the Chapel were practically exhausted when the bill for the digging came to us, and now it is becoming increasingly difficult to keep up with the costs. However, we know that the Merciful Jesus will not abandon us in the endeavor to honor Him for all the graces received through His Merciful Heart. This is best seen in the fact that Mr. Anthony Guerrieri—achitect and builder, who has two priest-sons and two daughters in the Convent, has come to aid us, despite the fact that our material means are wanting. His tireless efforts and hopes are indeed very encouraging to all, and it is quite gratifying to see him working side-by-side with everyone else.

## Build a Shrine

The original idea for the shrine began with Marian Helpers.

In the late 1940s, reader after reader of the *Marian Helpers Bulletin* (since renamed *Marian Helper* magazine) began contacting the Marians with the suggestion that a shrine be built specifically in thanksgiving for God's mercy. As it happened, this coincided with an internal need of the Marian community for a larger chapel on Eden Hill.

In May 1950, after much prayer and discussion, the superiors of the Marians in Stockbridge decided to build a shrine in thanks for the goodness God had shown them in their mission of spreading God's mercy. As recorded in the Marian archives, the Marians broke ground May 5 for the new Shrine of The Divine Mercy on a day that was "tranquil and bright." It took "five toilsome days" to dig out "a great, gaping hole."

The Marians hired local Stockbridge designer and builder Antonio Guerrieri, who, at 74, had just completed the renovations of St. Joseph Catholic Church in the center of Stockbridge. Amazingly, Guerrieri used no architectural plans or blueprints to build the Shrine.

*Brother Leonard Konopka, MIC (1933-2020), entered the Marian novitiate in 1951. During the '50s, he helped with the carving of some of the shrine's decorative wood pieces. He was trained by the shrine's designer Antonio Guerrieri, along with Stanley Olender, who also was considered one of the best carvers in the area.*

The Marians ran into many obstacles throughout this undertaking. Construction was laborious, and the limited means of the Congregation were practically exhausted to pay for the foundation work. As responsible stewards, the Marians only worked on the Shrine as funds permitted. Hence, the stop-and-go nature of construction through the 1950s.

Then, Guerrieri died before the chapel could be finished. As if that weren't enough, the Vatican placed a temporary ban on spreading the message of Divine Mercy in 1959 due to some faulty translations of St. Faustina's *Diary.* The Shrine was finally completed in 1960.

The ban on the devotion was lifted in 1978 by the Vatican's Congregation for the Doctrine of the Faith. In 1993, Pope John Paul II beatified Sister Faustina. In 1996, the United States Conference of Catholic Bishops officially designated the Shrine as "the National Shrine of The Divine Mercy."

Ever since Pope John Paul II canonized St. Faustina and established the Feast of Divine Mercy in 2000, the Shrine has been visited by tens of thousands of pilgrims every year. It is now host to the largest annual Divine Mercy Sunday celebration in North America.

*Father Anthony Gramlich, MIC, rector of the National Shrine of The Divine Mercy, says he chose the Marians of the Immaculate Conception because of his devotion to the Blessed Mother, who leads souls to her merciful Son.*

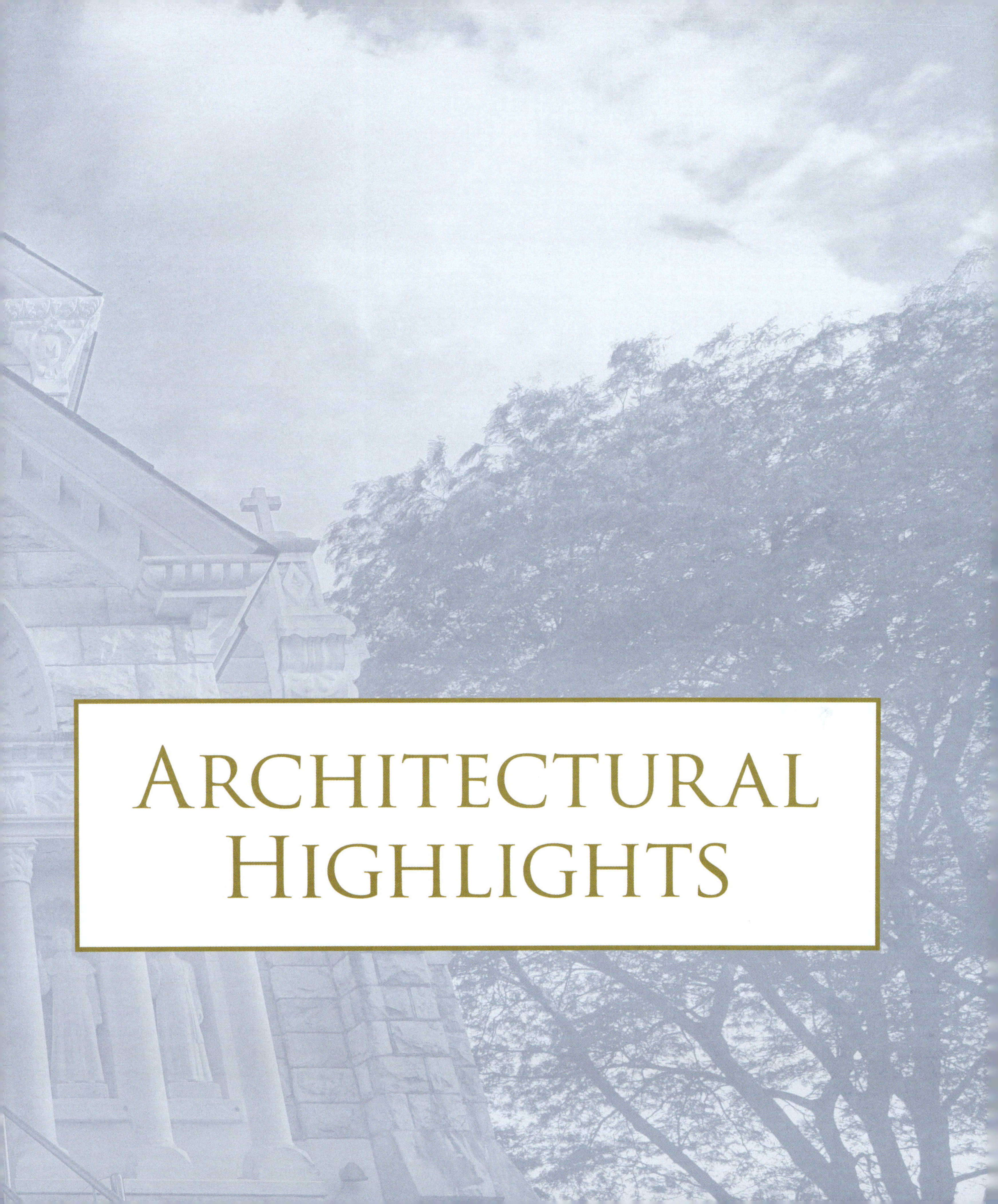

# Architectural Highlights

The National Shrine was built in honor of Jesus (The Divine Mercy) and Mary Immaculate. Like most Marian shrines, the National Shrine is a center of intense Christian life that promotes the Liturgy and the Sacraments. God uses Mary to save souls. She stands ready to hear our prayer petitions and to draw us into a deeper relationship with her divine Son.

***Main Altar***

The main altar is made of Vermont marble and it holds the tabernacle for reserving the Eucharist. Above the altar stands the Divine Mercy Image, which is flanked by hand-carved statues of the apostles by Fernando Peratrones of northern Italy. And, just above the Divine Mercy Image is a statue of Mary the Immaculate Conception carved from white Carrara marble. A magnificent mural above the statue depicts the Father, the Son, and the Holy Spirit, crowning her as Queen of Heaven and Earth.

***Rose Window***

Looking to the choir loft, a grand rose window depicts various symbols of Mary and of the Church's liturgical life.

JESUS I TRUST IN YOU

***Brickwork***
Each brick and stone was positioned by hand or by using a hand-powered rope-and-pully.

***Stained-Glass Windows***

The "Good Samaritan" is one of 14 windows that line the side walls of the Shrine, each depicting a Gospel scene that demonstrates the mercy of God. The Shrine features 36 stained-glass windows and two mosaics created by artist Fred Leuchs of Stockbridge.

OUR LADY OF
CZESTOCHOWA
DONUM JOSEPHÆ DLUGOSZ

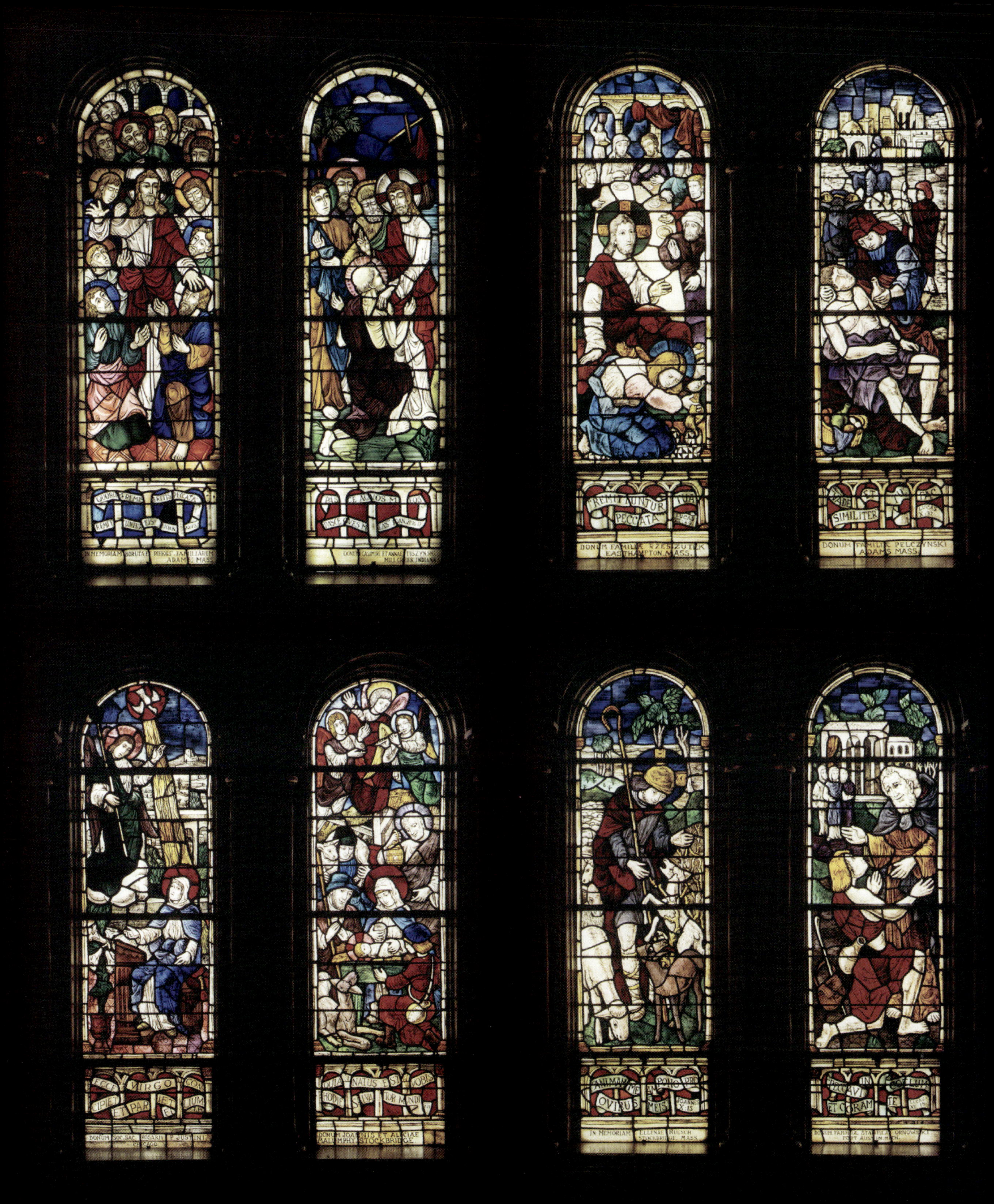
IN MEMORIAM
PASCE OVES
DONUM FAMILIAE PELCZYNSKI
ADAMS MASS.
PECCATA
SIMILITER
EASTHAMPTON MASS.
ECCE VIRGO
ET PAR
DONUM SOC. SAC.
QUIA NATUS EST VOBIS
DONUM JOANNIS ET
STOCKBRIDGE
JOANNES X:15
IN MEMORIAM
STOCKBRIDGE MASS.
ET CORAM

OUR LADY OF WILNO
DONUM PAULINÆ WILENTA
S. JOANNES EV.
DONUM REV. JOANNIS P. SKOWRONSKI HOUSATONIC, MASS
S. MARCUS EV.
DONUM DOROTHEAE HULSEMAN, MINNETKA ILL

***Carved Wood Confessional***

The Sacrament of Reconciliation is one of the ways we receive God's mercy. Here souls are cleansed and revived. As Jesus revealed to St. Faustina, "There the greatest miracles take place [and] are incessantly repeated" (*Diary*, 1448).

I
II
III
IV
V
VI
VII
VIII
IX

*Stations of the Cross*
The 14 Stations of the Cross were handcrafted in Spain.

JESUS I TRUST IN YOU

# Interior Highlights

### *Divine Mercy Image*

Located just above the tabernacle, this new Divine Mercy Image was installed during the renovation of the Shrine in early 2020 and blessed on the 60th anniversary of the dedication of the Shrine on May 30, 2020.

It is an enhanced digitized version of the Vilnius Image — the original Image that was painted by artist Eugene Kazimirowski under the direction of St. Faustina. In 1931, our Lord appeared to St. Faustina. She saw Jesus clothed in a white garment with His right hand raised in blessing. His left hand was touching His garment in the area of the Heart, from where two large rays came forth, one red and the other pale. Jesus said to her, **"Paint an image according to the pattern you see, with the signature: Jesus, I trust in You. I promise that the soul that will venerate this image will not perish. I also promise victory over [its] enemies already here on earth, especially at the hour of death. I Myself will defend it as My own glory** (*Diary*, 47-48).

JESUS I TRUST IN YOU
SAINT JOHN

***The Coronation of Mary Stained Glass***
Located above the entrance doors, this beautiful window is one of the many works of stained glass done for the Shrine by artist Fred Leuchs.

***St. Joseph Chapel***

Located to the left of the main altar, the St. Joseph Chapel honors the man to whom God the Father entrusted the protection of His only Begotten Son. Despite what this responsibility entailed for St. Joseph — nothing less than the radical redirection of his life — he responded with faith to become the protector and guardian of the Holy Family. Like St. Joseph, who is one of the patrons of the Marian Congregation, the Marians have hearts full of love and sacrifice, choosing to do their work quietly for the good of the Church, for the good of the community, with their main focus on ensuring that Jesus be better known and loved.

***St. Faustina Chapel***

In her *Diary,* 441, St. Maria Faustina Kowalska records a vision during the exposition of the Blessed Sacrament. She saw the rays of mercy extend from the Divine Mercy Image through the Host, and she heard the words: **"These rays of mercy will pass through you, just as they have passed through this Host, and they will go out through all the world."**

The bas relief in this chapel captures this experience, which characterizes her mission. Installed Aug. 8, 1993, it was carved by Fernando Peratrones.

In front of the artwork are two first-class relics, specifically, from the basal phalanx of a great toe of St. Faustina, who died in 1938.

Pictured above is the upper reliquary — two angels holding the relic, like bearers of gifts — was made at the instruction of Fr. Seraphim Michalenko, MIC, who served as vice-postulator in North America for St. Faustina's canonization cause.

Within the kneeler is a piece of that same bone. The Marians decided to separate this small piece of the relic to make it more accessible to the many pilgrims who wish to venerate it. Every day at the Shrine, pilgrims pray to St. Faustina, who wrote that her mission would continue after her death.

"Through you,
as through
this Host,
the rays of mercy
will pass to
the world."

***St. Stanislaus Papczynski Alcove*** *(left)*

The Marian Founder, St. Stanislaus of Jesus and Mary Papczynski (1631-1701), was canonized on June 5, 2016. This alcove has a kneeler with a first-class relic of St. Stanislaus. The canonization miracle through his intercession involved the healing of a 20-year-old Polish woman in 2007. The woman had developed acute respiratory distress syndrome, multiple organ failure, and septic shock. Her doctors had no hope for her recovery. Her family prayed a novena through Blessed Stanislaus' intercession. A little over a month later, she was released from the hospital, with no signs of damage to her lungs. This miracle is one of the reasons why the Holy See has assigned St. Stanislaus with the title "Patron Saint of Those in Mortal Danger."

***St. John Paul II Alcove*** *(right)*

Pope John Paul II was a long-time supporter of the Marians in their mission to spread the message of Divine Mercy. "Be Apostles of Divine Mercy under the maternal and loving guidance of Mary," he told them on June 22, 1993.

As a tangible sign of his closeness to the Marians, he offered his zucchetto (a skullcap) to the National Shrine on June 2, 2000. In this same side altar, pilgrims also may venerate a first-class relic of St. John Paul II encased in the marble kneeler before an image of the beloved pontiff.

***Murals***

Murals and paintings extend throughout the upper walls of the Shrine.

*Above:* Following the beatification of Marian Founder Stanislaus Papczynski on Sept. 16, 2007, local artist Laurel A. Tewes was asked to add a halo to the mural of the "Apostolic Approval of the Marians," which has been part of the Shrine since its completion in 1960. The Marian Founder was later canonized on June 5, 2016.

*Top right:* By 1909, extreme persecution reduced the Marian community down to one member: Fr. Vincent Senkowski, shown kneeling on the right. He is handing on the charism of the Marians to Blessed George Matulaitis-Matulewicz who joined the community secretly and renovated it. Pope Pius X (center) is giving his papal blessing for the newly renovated community.

*Bottom right:* The Lamb of God mural on the front ceiling is one of many painted by Joseph Amato of Bridgeport, Connecticut, before the Shrine's completion in 1960. Why a lamb? Before agreeing to baptize Christ, John the Baptist, pointed Him out to his disciples, saying "Behold, the Lamb of God, who takes away the sin of the world" (Jn 1:29). He is also the Paschal Lamb, the symbol of Israel's redemption at the first Passover.

# Interior of the National Shrine of the Divine Mercy

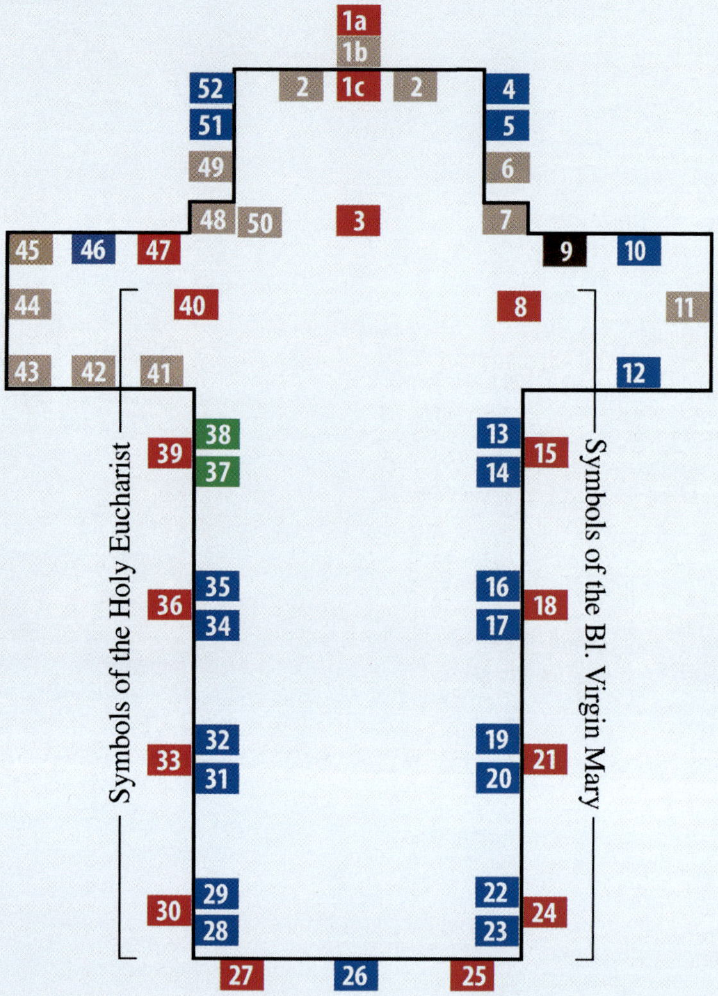


**Stained Glass**
**Statues & Carvings**
**Paintings & Murals**
**Mosaics**
**Display**

- 1a The Holy Trinity (top to bottom)
- 1b Immaculate Conception
- 1c Divine Mercy
- 2 The 12 Apostles: (left to right)
  St. Jude
  St. Phillip
  St. Matthias
  St. James the Lesser
  St. Matthew
  St. Peter
  St. John
  St. James the Greater
  St. Bartholomew
  St. Andrew
  St. Thomas
  St. Simon
- 3 The Lamb of God (ceiling)
- 4 Presentation of Jesus
- 5 Flight Into Egypt
- 6 Statue & 1st Class Relic of St. John Paul II
- 7 St. Michael
- 8 Apostolic Approval of the Marians
- 9 St. John Paul II Zuchetto & Rosary
- 10 Our Lady of Vilnius
- 11 St. Maria Faustina Kowalska Re
- 12 St. Margaret Mary Alacoque
- 13 The Annunciation
- 14 The Nativity
- 15 St. Paul
- 16 Parable of the Lost Sheep
- 17 Parable of the Prodigal Son
- 18 St. Thomas Aquinas
- 19 The Sinful Woman
- 20 Parable of the Good Samaritan
- 21 St. Ignatius of Loyola
- 22 The Last Supper
- 23 The Crucifixion
- 24 St. Joan of France
- 25 Our Lady of Czestochowa
- 26 Rose Window of the BVM
- 27 Our Lady of Vilnius
- 28 Piercing of the Sacred Heart
- 29 Our Lady of Sorrows (The Pieta)
- 30 St. Vincent de Paul
- 31 Sacrament of Reconciliation
- 32 Christ Commisions St. Peter (Feed My Sheep)
- 33 St. Francis of Assisi
- 34 Pentecost
- 35 Conversion of St. Paul
- 36 St. Michael the Archangel
- 37 St. Thomas' Confession of Faith
- 38 The Disciples of Emmaus
- 39 St. Peter
- 40 Renovation of the Marian Congregation
- 41 Bl. Anthony Leszczewicz & Bl. George Kaszyra
- 42 Bl. George Matulaitis-Matulewicz
- 43 St. Thérése
- 44 St. Joseph with Child Jesus
- 45 Our Lady of Fatima
- 46 Our Lady of Czestochowa
- 47 Purgatory Icon
- 48 Crucifix
- 49 Statue & 1st Class Relic of St. Stanislaus Papczynski (Founder of the Marian Fathers)
- 50 Infant of Prague
- 51 The Finding of Jesus in the Temple
- 52 The Holy Family

JESUS I TRUST IN YOU

# WALKING TOUR

IMMACULATA VIRGINIS MARIAE CONCEPTIO
SIT NOBIS SALUS ET PROTECTIO

*Our Lady of Eden Hill*
This statue of the Immaculate Conception was one of the first landmarks the Marians erected here. They entrusted the property and their work to the Blessed Virgin Mary under the title Our Lady of Eden Hill. Below the statue is the motto of the Marian founder, St. Stanislaus Papczynski, "May the Virgin Mary's Immaculate Conception be our health and protection."

***St. John Paul II Plaza***

At the shrine office entrance stands a life-size bronze statue of St. John Paul II with arms outstretched in a gesture of welcome to all.

On June 7, 1997, at the Shrine of Divine Mercy in Krakow, Poland, the pontiff announced, "There is nothing the world needs more than Divine Mercy."

Father Seraphim Michalenko, MIC, a life-long Divine Mercy scholar, said Pope John Paul II took the revelations of St. Faustina so seriously because he knew the revelations of Divine Mercy were particularly tailored to our times. At an audience with the Holy Father on Aug. 17, 2002, in Krakow, Poland, Fr. Seraphim thanked the Pope for his tireless work on behalf of Divine Mercy, including the canonization of Sr. Faustina two years earlier. The Holy Father returned the compliment, noting Fr. Seraphim's role as vice postulator of the saint's cause.

The plaza, unveiled on Oct. 22, 2012, is a reminder of the task the Holy Father entrusted to the Marians — "be apostles of Divine Mercy…" — and for those who assist them in their mission.

***Statue of St. Maria Faustina Kowalska***

Saint Faustina was a young, undereducated religious sister of the Congregation of Sisters of Our Lady of Mercy in Poland. She received visions of the Lord Jesus in the 1930s, which she recorded in her *Diary*. Jesus gave her the title "Secretary" of Divine Mercy. On April 30, 2000, St. John Paul II canonized her as the first saint of the new millennium and announced that the Second Sunday of Easter would now be known as Divine Mercy Sunday. This marble statue depicts St. Faustina kneeling before Jesus, the Divine Mercy, as He appeared to her on Feb. 22, 1931. It was commissioned from Drapikowski Studio in Poland. The original statue is at the Cathedral of St. Stanislaus Kostka in Lodz, Poland, the site where St. Faustina prayed after seeing a vision of the suffering Jesus calling her to a religious vocation (see *Diary*, 9).

# Life-Size Stations of the Cross

Eden Hill's life-size Stations of the Cross are the accomplishment of world-renowned Christian sculptor Timothy P. Schmalz of Ontario, Canada, who spent three years working on this project. It consists of 52 life-size figures and 13 crosses.

In Church tradition, meditating on the Paschal mystery through the Stations of the Cross has served as a means by which we can surrender ourselves more deeply to our merciful Lord, who accepted the Cross for the salvation of mankind. Through the private revelations of St. Maria Faustina Kowalska (1905-1938), Christ tells us, **"You please Me most when you meditate on My Sorrowful Passion"** (*Diary*, 1512).

I

II

III

IV

V

VI

VI

VII

VIII

IX

X

XI

XII

XIII

XIV

***Statue of Blessed George Matulaitis-Matulewicz***

Without the Marian Renovator Blessed George Matulaitis-Matulewicz, the Marian Fathers might not exist today. In 1909, the Marian Fathers of the Immaculate Conception had dwindled down to just one member as a result of persecution of religious orders in Russia. Blessed George famously prayed that the Lord make him a "dishrag" to clean the Church, to be worn out and thrown away when his mission was over. He revised the Congregation's Constitutions and formed an underground seminary program. From there, the Marians expanded. In 1913, he brought the Marians to the United States. He was appointed Bishop of Vilnius, Lithuania, in 1918. He died on Jan. 27, 1927. Visit BlessedGeorge.org to learn more.

***Grotto of Our Lady of Lourdes / Immaculate Conception Candle Shrine***

The Marian Fathers became the first male religious community founded under the title of the Immaculate Conception — nearly 200 years before the declaration of the dogma. Located down a narrow path on Eden Hill is a special tribute to the Blessed Virgin Mary under this title.

In the 1950s, the Marians built a replica of the original grotto where Our Lady appeared to a peasant girl in 1858 in Lourdes, France. Saint Bernadette Soubirous was 14 years old when the Blessed Virgin Mary appeared to her 18 times in the Grotto at Massabielle. Our Lady told St. Bernadette, "I am the Immaculate Conception."

Opposite the Grotto of Our Lady of Lourdes is the Immaculate Conception Candle Shrine. This shrine is dedicated to the Holy Souls in Purgatory. Praying for the Holy Souls is one of the founding charisms of the Marian Fathers. The shrine's alcoves illustrate the Church's teaching on Purgatory, especially our call to pray for our deceased loved ones.

MA
RIA

*Mosaics at the Immaculate Conception Candle Shrine depict (from left) Christ drawing souls into the heavenly glory of the Most Holy Trinity, and experiences of Purgatory by St. Stanislaus Papczynski and St. Faustina.*

***Mother of Mercy Outdoor Shrine***
Located on the hill behind the National Shrine, the Mother of Mercy Outdoor Shrine provides a protected, respectful setting for the celebration of the Eucharist on Divine Mercy Sunday and other feast days where the number of pilgrims exceeds seating within the National Shrine. The stained-glass windows on the wings of the façade depict the Seven Joys and Sorrows of Our Lady. On the center façade, different elements show the connection between the Divine Mercy message and the Marian Fathers of the Immaculate Conception.

### *Shrine of the Holy Innocents*

The decision on how to design the lower level of the Mother of Mercy Outdoor Shrine fell upon Fr. Anthony Gramlich, MIC, the rector of the Shrine in the 2010s. Ever since he had been a seminarian, Fr. Anthony dreamed of creating a pro-life shrine to honor deceased children.

The Shrine of the Holy Innocents centers around a life-size statue of Our Lady of Guadalupe, the Patroness of Life, depicted carrying the Child Jesus in her womb. Thirteen-foot tall bronze cherubim angels guard the entrance to the shrine where these children are remembered. Opening the doors, one can hear heavenly music and the sound of water falling gently down mosaic walls. A pathway of bronze baby footprints leads to Our Lady and St. Joseph. The names of deceased children are etched upon tiles decorating this shrine. Interspersed among the tiles are beautiful images and Scripture passages as reminders of God's promise of eternal life.

For those who suffer the painful loss of a child, it is a place of healing.

***Holy Family Shrine***

The basic structure of the Holy Family Shrine was a feature of the estate when the Marians purchased the property in 1943. It originally served as a garden with a marble statue of St. Joseph holding Baby Jesus in the portico. Today, with the addition of a marble statue of the Holy Family, it honors the dignity and importance of families. Pilgrims find it to be a peaceful place to meditate on Jesus, Mary, and Joseph and invoke their intercession. Many create memorials to remember family members or commemorate special occasions. Memorials are carved in pavers surrounding the shrine or etched on the blue stained-glass windows.

***Statue of St. Stanislaus Papczynski and the Marian Cemetery***

Saint Stanislaus of Jesus and Mary Papczynski (1631-1701) founded the Marian Fathers in 1670. The Marian Fathers became the first male religious order founded in Poland and the first under the title of the Immaculate Conception — nearly two centuries before the dogma would be proclaimed by the Church.

The Marians' charism has three essential points: promoting the Mystery of the Immaculate Conception, praying for the Holy Souls in Purgatory and for the dying, and serving Christ and the Church where the need is greatest.

Living in a war-torn time period, St. Stanislaus witnessed thousands of casualties on battlefields and also from dreaded plagues. He accompanied Polish troops as a chaplain in battles against Turkey in Ukraine in 1674. He was deeply saddened to observe how many people died with no time to prepare to meet their Maker. After he experienced visions of the Holy Souls in Purgatory, he was moved to engage in, and advocate for, prayer and penance on their behalf.

Because of St. Stanislaus' devotion to the Holy Souls, his bronze statue stands across from the Marian Cemetery.

***St. Faustina Center***

The St. Faustina Center was completed in 2016 in a former recreational building. It plays host to special events, conferences, and talks given by the Marian Fathers and guest speakers.

***Divine Mercy Gift Shop***

This building was once a barn, then a recreational center. Today, it holds the largest Catholic gift shop in New England. You will find an extensive collection of books, CDs, DVDs, religious art, rosaries, jewelry, and gift items.

***St. John Paul II House***

The St. John Paul II House offers a limited number of basic, but clean and comfortable accommodations giving pilgrims an opportunity for spiritual renewal. Each room is named after a saint or special devotions. The house also offers a shared library/sitting room. Although meals are not provided, pilgrims have access to a shared kitchen and may bring their own food for their stay.

***Marian Helpers Center***

The Marian Helpers Center publishes several million pieces of religious materials each year, many of which are sent around the world.

It also serves as the headquarters of the Association of Marian Helpers (AMH), which was established in 1944 as a spiritual benefit society. The prayers and support of more than one million members benefit the Marians' apostolic works around the world.

By 1959, to meet the demand for the printed word the Marians converted the estate's old carriage barn into a press department. In 1963, continued growth of the ministry led to a new building being added to the old horse barn. With various additions and renovations over the years, the barn still houses the printing presses on the first floor.

***Divine Mercy Statue***

This statue of Jesus greets pilgrims as they enter Eden Hill. It was given to honor Divine Mercy, and to memorialize Katherine Wilbanks Garvey and Col. Joseph Patrick Garvey and the victims of the terrorist attacks on Sept. 11, 2001.

It is a smaller version of the same bronze statue at the Shrine of Our Lady of Kibeho in Rwanda, which was installed after the genocide in the 1980s. Both statues were designed by Mexican artist Gogi Farias.

These Divine Mercy statues remind us to pray for peace and an end to violence in the world. Beside the Eden Hill statue is an engraving of a quote from Jesus to St. Faustina: "Mankind will not have peace until it turns with trust My mercy" (*Diary*, 300).

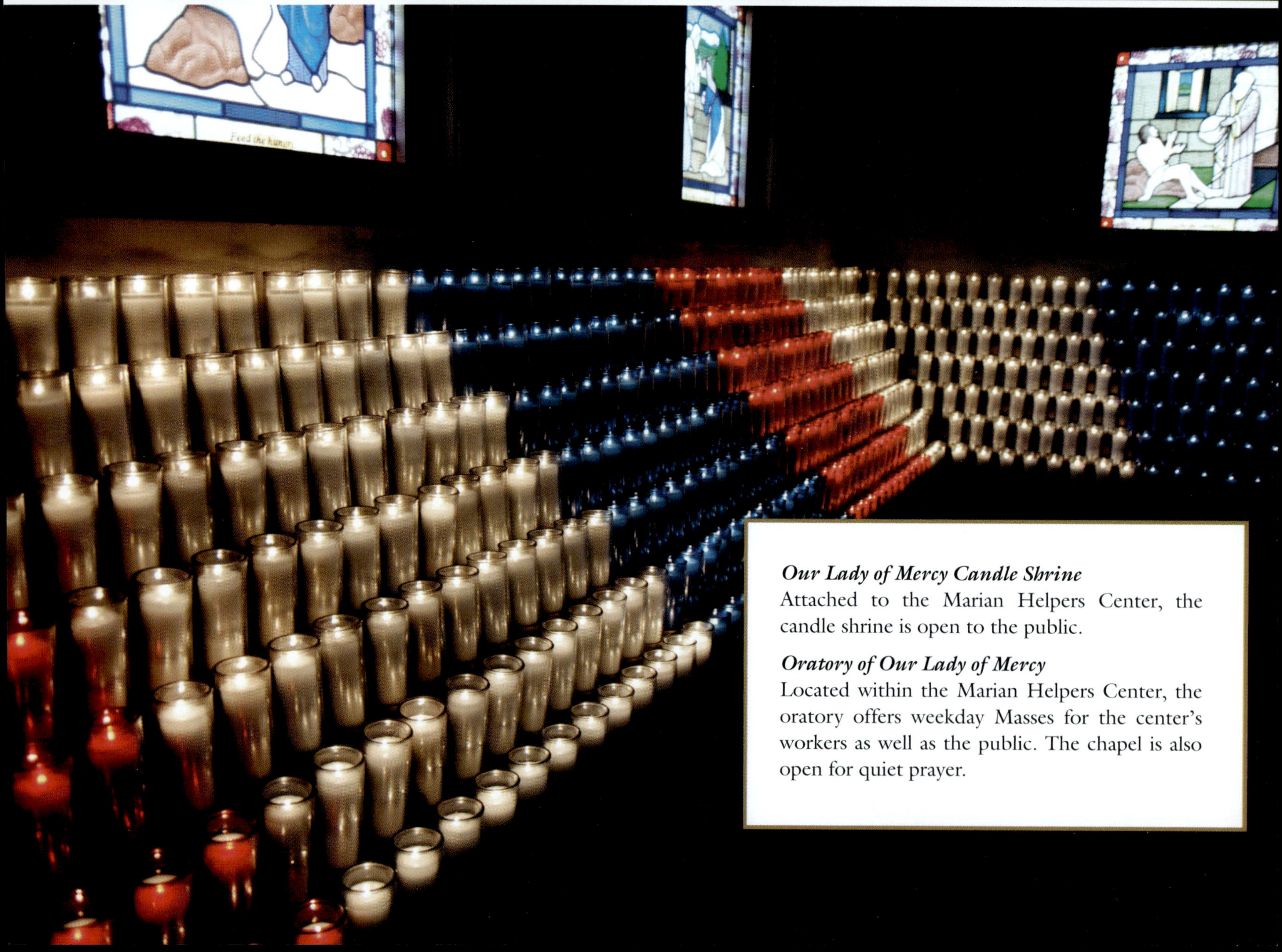

***Our Lady of Mercy Candle Shrine***
Attached to the Marian Helpers Center, the candle shrine is open to the public.

***Oratory of Our Lady of Mercy***
Located within the Marian Helpers Center, the oratory offers weekday Masses for the center's workers as well as the public. The chapel is also open for quiet prayer.

O BLOOD AND WATER

# Additional Statues

**St. Peregrine** — The patron saint of those suffering from cancer. Saint Peregrine's Knoll has become a special place of prayer, particularly for people suffering from serious illness. The Marian Fathers offer an annual novena through his intercession before his feast day, July 27.

**St. Thérèse of Lisieux** — a 19th century French Carmelite who would become the youngest Doctor of the Church. Author Fr. Michael Gaitley, MIC, calls her consecration to Divine Mercy "the culmination of her whole spiritual teaching on the Little Way, the crowning of her path to holiness."

**St. Francis of Assisi** — a patron saint of the Marian Fathers. The Marians were originally founded under a Franciscan rule, the *Rule of the Ten Evangelical Virtues of the Blessed Virgin Mary.*

**St. Joseph** — the patron saint of the universal Church, which abides under his fatherly care and protection. He is a patron saint of the Marian Fathers who, through his example and intercession, helps them faithfully fulfill the will of God. Saint Joseph also is the patron saint of workers.

**St. Philomena** — a fourth century consecrated virgin martyred at the age of 13. She's the patron saint of youth and priests.

**St. Anthony of Padua** — a Franciscan brother who lived around the time of St. Francis. Noted for his care for the poor, he is also the patron saint of lost and stolen articles.

**Our Lady, Comfort of Novices** — a statue from the original house on Eden Hill, which was designated as a novitiate, that is, the initial program of formation where candidates discern a religious vocation.

**Sacred Heart of Jesus** — a statue of Christ, the Redeemer of the World. It stands on a marble pedestal, 12 feet above the ground. His arms are raised, extending a blessing to the whole world. It was erected in 1947.

1
2
3
4
5
6
7
8
12
14
15
16
17
18
19
20
21
22
23
24
25
E
S
W
N

# MAP OF EDEN HILL

1. Our Lady of Mercy Candle Shrine and Oratory
2. Marian Helpers Center
3. Gift Shop
4. St. John Paul II House
5. The Divine Mercy Statue
6. Marian Cemetery
7. St. Joseph/Holy Family Candle Shrine
8. St. Anthony of Padua Statue
9. Mother of Mercy Outdoor Shrine
10. Shrine of the Holy Innocents
11. St. Joseph and the Baby Jesus Statue
12. St. Thérèse of Liseux Statue
13. Lourdes Grotto and Immaculate Conception Candle Shrine
14. Our Lady, Comfort of Novices Statue
15. St. Philomena Statue/Relic
16. Bl. George Matulaitis-Matulewicz Statue
17. St. Peregrine's Knoll
18. Way of the Cross
19. National Shrine of the Divine Mercy
20. St. Faustina Plaza
21. St. John Paul II Plaza
22. St. Francis Grove
23. Our Lady of Eden Hill Fountain
24. St. Stanislaus Papczynski Statue
25. Oblate Sisters Convent

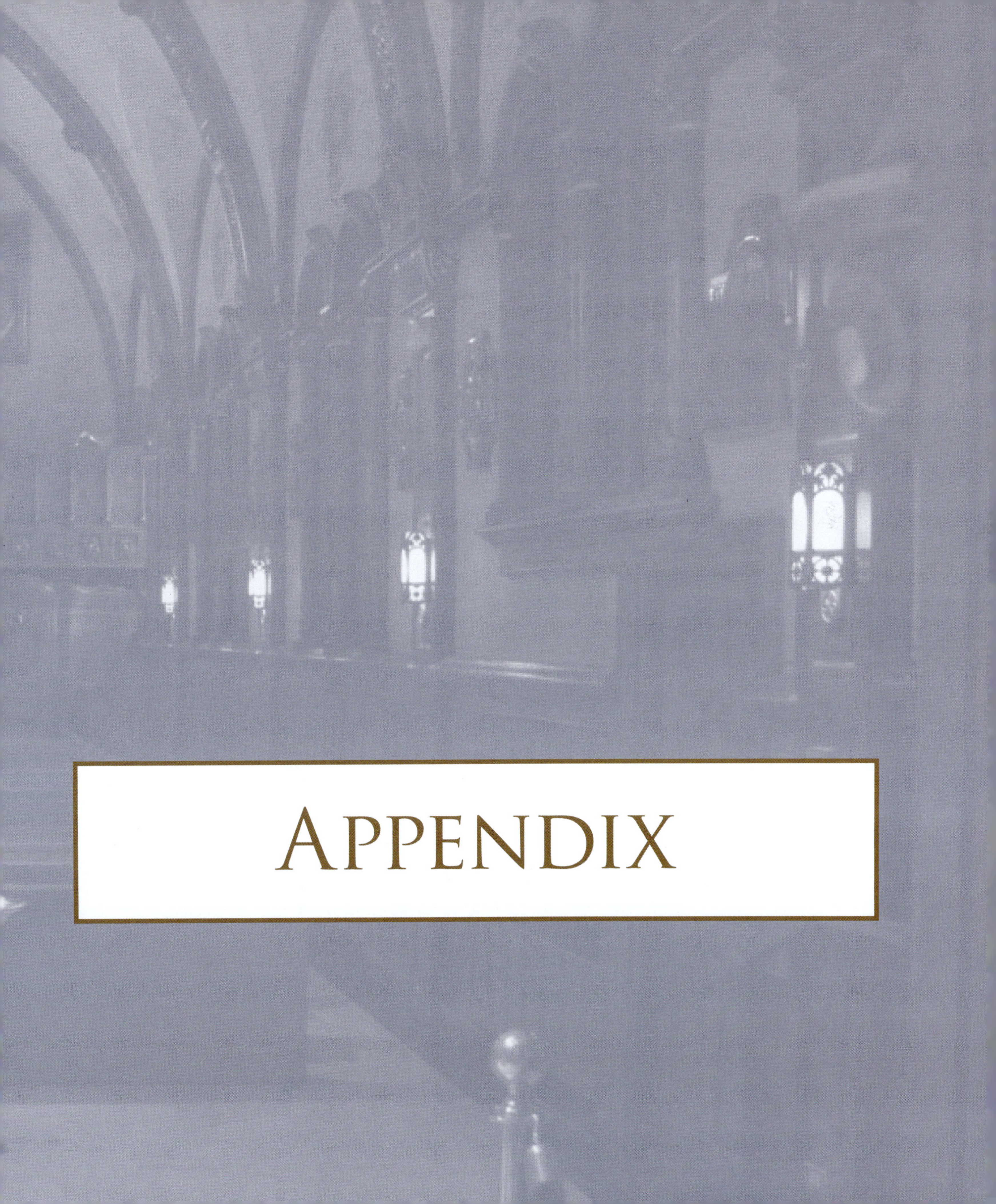

# APPENDIX

JESUS I TRUST IN YOU

## Daily Devotions / Hour of Great Mercy

Every day, when the shrine bell rings in the three o'clock hour, Marian priests and religious, Shrine staff, and pilgrims from around the world gather to offer a special prayer: the Chaplet of Divine Mercy. They do so in response to Jesus' request as recorded in the *Diary of Saint Maria Faustina Kowalska*:

> **At three o'clock, implore My mercy, especially for sinners; and, if only for a brief moment, immerse yourself in My Passion, particularly in My abandonment at the moment of agony. This is the Hour of Great Mercy for the whole world. ... In this hour I will refuse nothing to the soul that makes a request of Me in virtue of My Passion ...**(1320).

In His revelations to St. Faustina, our Lord asked for special prayer and meditation on His Passion each afternoon at the three o'clock hour, the hour that recalls His death on the Cross:

> **... try your best to make the Stations of the Cross in this hour, provided that your duties permit it; and if you are not able to make the Stations of the Cross, then at least step into the chapel for a moment and adore, in the Most Blessed Sacrament, My Heart, which is full of mercy; and should you be unable to step into the chapel, immerse yourself in prayer there where you happen to be, if only for a very brief instant** (1572).

We may not all be able to make the Stations or adore Him in the Blessed Sacrament, but we can all mentally pause for a "brief moment" to recall His hour of agony and say a short prayer such as "Jesus, mercy."

The Chaplet of Divine Mercy is especially appropriate at this hour. It can help us to dwell on the wounds of our Lord while we use the five decades of our rosary beads.

In 1935, St. Faustina received inspiration to offer this prayer. In subsequent revelations, He made it clear that the Chaplet was not just for her, but for the whole world. He also attached extraordinary promises to its recitation:

> **... encourage souls to say the chaplet which I have given you** (1541).

> **Whoever will recite it will receive great mercy at the hour of death** (687).

> **... when they say this chaplet in the presence of the dying, I will stand between My Father and the dying person, not as the just Judge but as the Merciful Savior** (1541).

> **Even if there were a sinner most hardened, if he were to recite this chaplet only once, he would receive grace from My infinite mercy** (687).

> **Through the chaplet you will obtain everything, if what you ask for is compatible with My will** (1731).

The Divine Mercy Chaplet is an intercessory prayer that extends the offering of the Eucharist, so it is especially appropriate to pray it after having received Holy Communion. It may be said at any time, but our Lord also specifically told St. Faustina to recite it as a novena before Divine Mercy Sunday (the first Sunday after Easter). At the Shrine, the Chaplet is offered daily as a perpetual novena.

***Opening Prayers (optional)***
You expired, Jesus, but the source of life gushed forth for souls and the ocean of mercy opened up for the whole world. O Fount of Life, unfathomable Divine Mercy, envelop the whole world and empty Yourself out upon us (*Diary*, 1319).

O Blood and Water, which gushed forth from the Heart of Jesus as a fount of mercy for us, I trust in You (*Diary*, 84). **(three times)**

**The Our Father**

**The Hail Mary**

**The Apostles' Creed**

*Using the five decades of rosary beads, pray:*

**On the OUR FATHER BEADS**
V. Eternal Father, I offer You the Body and Blood, Soul and Divinity of Your dearly beloved Son, Our Lord Jesus Christ,

R. in atonement for our sins and those of the whole world.

**On the HAIL MARY BEADS**
V. For the sake of His sorrowful Passion,

R. Have mercy on us and on the whole world.

**In conclusion (three times):** Holy God, Holy Mighty One, Holy Immortal One, have mercy on us and on the whole world (*Diary*, 476).

***Closing Prayer***
Eternal God, in whom mercy is endless and the treasury of compassion inexhaustible, look kindly upon us and increase Your mercy in us, that in difficult moments we might not despair nor become despondent, but with great confidence submit ourselves to Your holy will, which is Love and Mercy itself (*Diary*, 950). Amen.

## Special Days

The Marian Fathers at the National Shrine of The Divine Mercy invite pilgrims to join them for special feast days, novenas, ethnic events, retreats, talks, and presentations.

Among the most attended days at the National Shrine are Divine Mercy Sunday and Encuentro Latino.

**Divine Mercy Sunday**

In a series of revelations to St. Maria Faustina Kowalska in the 1930s, our Lord called for a special feast day to be celebrated on the Sunday after Easter. Today, we know that feast as Divine Mercy Sunday, named by St. John Paul II at the canonization of St. Faustina on April 30, 2000.

In His very first revelation to St. Faustina, the Lord expressed His will with regard to this feast. The most comprehensive revelation can be found in her *Diary* entry 699:

> **My daughter, tell the whole world about My inconceivable mercy. I desire that the Feast of Mercy be a refuge and a shelter for all souls, and especially for poor sinners. On that day the very depths of My tender mercy are open. I pour out a whole ocean of graces upon those souls who approach the fount of My mercy. The soul that will go to Confession and receive Holy Communion shall obtain complete forgiveness of sins and punishment. On that day are opened all the divine floodgates through which graces flow. Let no soul fear to draw near to Me, even though its sins be as scarlet. ... The Feast of Mercy emerged from My very depths of tenderness. It is My desire that it be solemnly celebrated on the first Sunday after Easter.**

In all, St. Faustina recorded 14 revelations from Jesus concerning His desire for this feast. Nevertheless, Divine Mercy Sunday is *not* a feast based solely on St. Faustina's revelations. Indeed, it is not primarily about St. Faustina — nor is it altogether a new feast. The Second Sunday of Easter was already a solemnity as the Octave Day of Easter. The title "Divine Mercy Sunday" does, however, highlight the meaning of the day.

To receive the promised graces, go to Confession in preparation for the feast, remain in a state of grace to receive Communion on the feast. These graces also are available through the Saturday Vigil Mass. Veneration of the Divine Mercy Image is encouraged.

Pilgrims have long come to the National Shrine of The Divine Mercy to celebrate this feast. The shrine's celebration, the largest in North America, is traditionally broadcast on Eternal Word Television Network (EWTN).

**Encuentro Latino**

All events are in Spanish for this annual celebration in August. More than 5,000 faithful from different countries around the world come to the Shrine to praise God's mercy. Pilgrims enjoy a day of prayer and praise, dedicated to our Lord and His Blessed Mother.

The day includes spiritual presentations, a Rosary Procession, children's activities, music, and more. Holy Mass is celebrated at the Mother of Mercy Outdoor Shrine followed by the Chaplet of Divine Mercy and Benediction.

APOSTOLATE
UNION
NEW JERSEY

MOREL
ICE

EXIT
22

44
6

Viva
Cristo

POLISH COMMUNITY OF THE CHURCH
OF ST. MATTHIAS IN NEW YORK, A.D.2010.
MATKO NIEUSTAJĄCEJ POMOCY
OPIEKUJ SIĘ NAMI
OUR MOTHER OF PERPETUAL HELP
CARE FOR US

OF JESUS

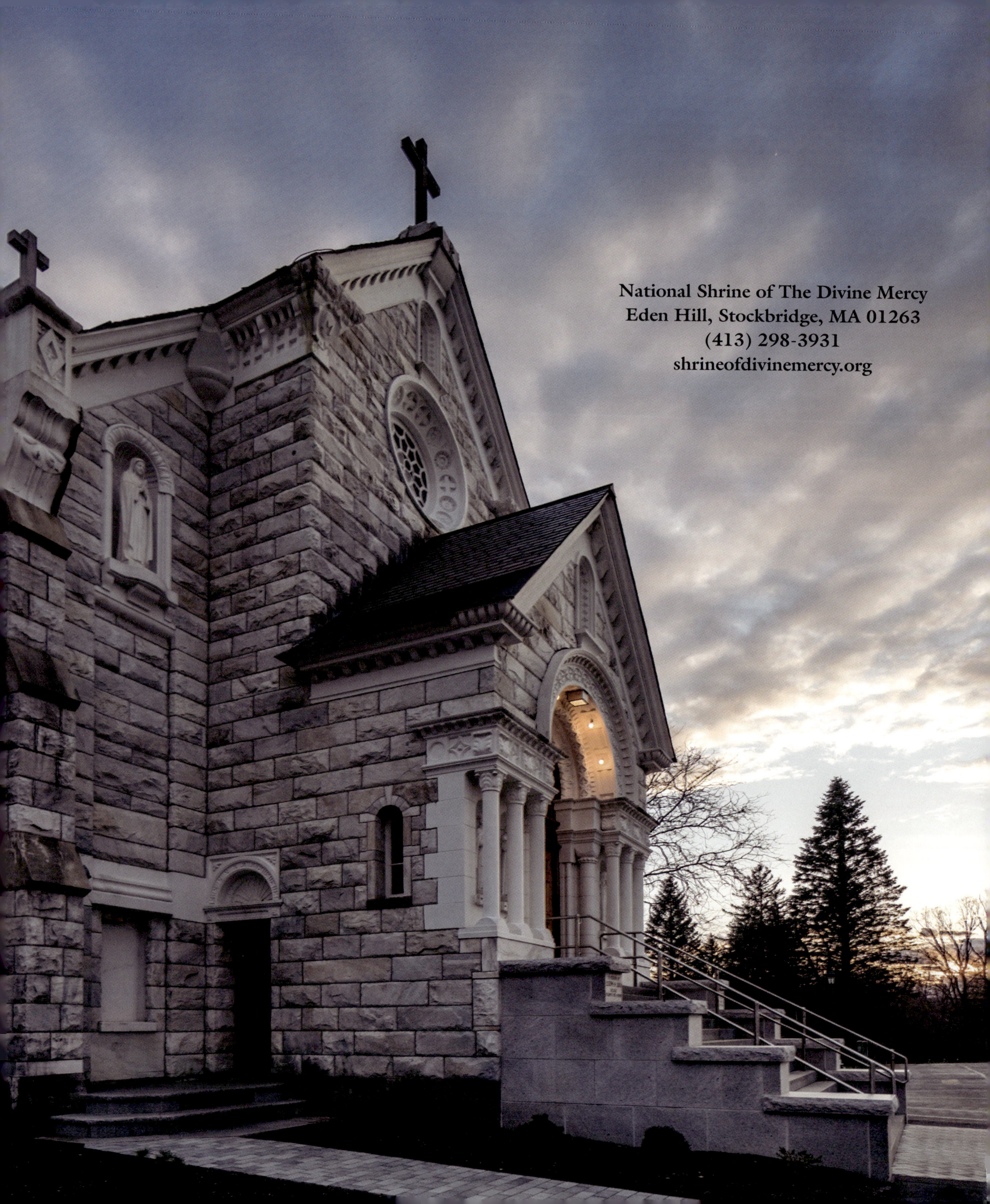
National Shrine of The Divine Mercy
Eden Hill, Stockbridge, MA 01263
(413) 298-3931
shrineofdivinemercy.org